First World War
and Army of Occupation
War Diary
France, Belgium and Germany

14 DIVISION
42 Infantry Brigade
Oxfordshire and Buckinghamshire Light Infantry
5th Battalion
18 May 1915 - 20 June 1918

WO95/1900/4

The Naval & Military Press Ltd
www.nmarchive.com
Published in association with The National Archives

Published by

The Naval & Military Press Ltd

Unit 10 Ridgewood Industrial Park,

Uckfield, East Sussex,

TN22 5QE England

Tel: +44 (0) 1825 749494

www.naval-military-press.com

www.nmarchive.com

This diary has been reprinted in facsimile from the original. Any imperfections are inevitably reproduced and the quality may fall short of modern type and cartographic standards.

© **Crown Copyright**
Images reproduced by permission of The National Archives, London, England, 2015.

Contents

Document type	Place/Title	Date From	Date To
Heading	WO95/1900/4 May 15 May 18 5 Bttn Ox Bucks Light Inf		
Heading	14th Division 42nd Infy Bde 6th Oxf & Bucks L.I. May 1915-Jun 1918		
War Diary	Aldershot	18/05/1915	20/05/1915
War Diary	Boulogne	21/05/1915	22/05/1915
War Diary	Rubrouck	23/05/1915	27/05/1915
War Diary	Steenvoorde	28/05/1915	30/05/1915
Heading	42nd Inf. Bde 14th Div. 5th Battn The Oxfordshire And Buckinghumshire Light Infantry. June 1915 (31.5 To 30.6.15)		
Heading			
War Diary	Huts Between Zeyecoten & La Clytte	31/05/1915	06/06/1915
War Diary	Dranoutre	07/06/1915	12/06/1915
War Diary	La Clytte	12/06/1915	14/06/1915
War Diary	Vlamertinghe	15/06/1915	19/06/1915
War Diary	Trenches At Railway Wood E Of Ypres.	20/06/1915	24/06/1915
War Diary	Billets Near Poperinghe	25/06/1915	30/06/1915
Miscellaneous	10 men with bombs		
Miscellaneous	5 Oxford Bucks Lt Infantry Order No. 1 Appendix 1		
Miscellaneous	Report On Attack Of Redoubt 42nd Inf Bde Appendix 2	22/06/1915	22/06/1915
Miscellaneous		23/06/1916	23/06/1916
Diagram etc	Plan Of Railway Wood Trenches		
Miscellaneous	O.C. 5th Oxf Buck L.I. Appendix 4	20/06/1915	20/06/1915
Miscellaneous	A Form. Messages And Signals.		
Operation(al) Order(s)	5th Oxford Bucks Lt Infantry Orders No.2 Appendix 5		
Miscellaneous	5th Ox & Bucks L. I. July 1915.		
Miscellaneous			
War Diary	Billets 3 Miles W. Of Poperinghe	01/07/1915	08/07/1915
War Diary	Railway Wood Trenches	09/07/1915	13/07/1915
War Diary	Ypres	14/07/1915	18/07/1915
War Diary	Camp G.17.d Sheet 28	19/07/1915	25/07/1915
War Diary	Near Poperinghe	26/07/1915	26/07/1915
War Diary	Railway Wood I. 11. B Sheet 28	28/07/1915	28/07/1915
War Diary	Railway Wood	29/07/1915	30/07/1915
War Diary	Railway Wood 1.11. b Sheet 28	30/07/1915	30/07/1915
War Diary	Railway Wood	30/07/1915	31/07/1915
Miscellaneous	A Form. Messages And Signals. Appx II		
Miscellaneous	Appx I Btn 7/131 5th Oxf Buck L.I.		
Miscellaneous	C Form (Original). Messages And Signals.		
Miscellaneous	A Form Messages And Signals.		
Miscellaneous	5th Oxford & Bucks I. 9. Appx V	19/07/1915	19/07/1915
Miscellaneous	Appen VI 5th Oxf Bucks L. I. 5th Shrops L I 9th K R R C 9th Rif Brig	23/07/1915	23/07/1915
Miscellaneous	C Form (Duplicate). Messages And Signals.		
Heading	14th Division 5th Ox. & Bucks. L.I. Vol. IV From 1-31.8.15		
War Diary	Railway Wood Ypres	01/08/1915	06/08/1915
War Diary	In Reserve	07/08/1915	09/08/1915

War Diary	Reserve		10/08/1915	10/08/1915
War Diary	Vlamertinghe		11/08/1915	20/08/1915
War Diary	Trenches E Of Ypres		21/08/1915	22/08/1915
War Diary	Trenches On Ypres Salient		23/08/1915	23/08/1915
War Diary	Vlamertinghe		24/08/1915	31/08/1915
Heading	14th Division 5th Ox And Bucks Vol 5 Sept 15			
War Diary	Camp Near Vlamertinghe		01/09/1915	07/09/1915
War Diary	Trenches Y Wood N. Of Hooge		08/09/1915	11/09/1915
War Diary	G.H.Q. Line Reserve		11/09/1915	15/09/1915
War Diary	Poperinghe		16/09/1915	23/09/1915
War Diary	L. Farm & Guards		24/09/1915	24/09/1915
War Diary	Poperinghe		26/09/1915	30/09/1915
Miscellaneous	K. Killed W. Wounded S. Sick Admitted To Hock.			
Miscellaneous	K. Killed W. Wounded S. Sick Admitted To Hospital			
Miscellaneous	Messages And Signals.			
Miscellaneous	To D.A.G. 3rd Echelon		02/10/1915	02/10/1915
Miscellaneous	Special Report On Operations Of 25th Sept. 1915			
Miscellaneous	5th Bn. Oxf. & Bucks. Light Infty. Operation Orders.		22/09/1915	22/09/1915
Miscellaneous	5th Bn. Oxf. & Bucks. Light Infty. Operation Orders.		24/09/1915	24/09/1915
Miscellaneous	5th Bn. Oxf. & Bucks. Light Infty. Report On Action Of 25th September 1915		25/09/1915	25/09/1915
Miscellaneous	5th Bn. Oxf. & Bucks. Light Infty. Report On Operation By Barwell, D.2 25th Sept. 15		25/09/1915	25/09/1915
Miscellaneous	5th Bn. Oxf. & Bucks. Light Infty.			
Diagram etc	Sketch Of Bellevarde Trenches			
Map	German Line			
Heading	14th Division 5th Ox. & Bucks Vol 6 Oct 15			
War Diary	Camp Near Poperinghe		01/10/1915	13/10/1915
War Diary	Railway Wood Trenches		13/10/1915	19/10/1915
War Diary	L.4 Seminaire Nr Ypres		20/10/1915	22/10/1915
War Diary	Herzeele		23/10/1915	31/10/1915
Miscellaneous	5th (S) Bn Oxford & Bucks Lt Infty			
Heading	14th Division 5th Ox & Bucks Li. Vol. 7 Nov 15			
War Diary	Herzeele		01/11/1915	19/11/1915
War Diary	B Huts G.6.d Sheet 28		20/11/1915	20/11/1915
War Diary	Ypres		21/11/1915	26/11/1915
War Diary	G.6.d Sheet 25		27/11/1915	27/11/1915
War Diary	Potijze 14 (Sheet 28)		28/11/1915	30/11/1915
War Diary	Kaaie		01/12/1915	02/12/1915
Heading	5th Ox & Bucks Vol 8 27th Nov 31st Nov Dec			
War Diary	Brandhoek		27/11/1915	27/11/1915
War Diary	Potijze		28/11/1915	30/11/1915
War Diary	Kaaie		01/12/1915	02/12/1915
War Diary	Potijze		03/12/1915	05/12/1915
War Diary	Kaaie		06/12/1915	08/12/1915
War Diary	Potijze		09/12/1915	12/12/1915
War Diary	Sheet 28 B Camp (F27)		13/12/1915	13/12/1915
War Diary	B. Camp		14/12/1915	14/12/1915
War Diary	Herzeele		15/12/1915	29/12/1915
War Diary	B Huts		30/12/1915	30/12/1915
War Diary	St. Jean		31/12/1915	31/12/1915
Heading	5th Ox & Bucks Li Vol. 9			
War Diary	St Jean		01/01/1916	03/01/1916
War Diary	A 30		04/01/1916	05/01/1916
War Diary	A. 16 C.		06/01/1916	08/01/1916
War Diary	Elverdinghe		09/01/1916	11/01/1916

War Diary	St. Jean	12/01/1916	14/01/1916
War Diary	B Huts	15/01/1916	19/01/1916
War Diary	Elverdinghe	20/01/1916	23/01/1916
War Diary	St Jean	24/01/1916	27/01/1916
War Diary	B. Huts	28/01/1916	31/01/1916
Heading	5th Ox & Bucks Vol 10 14th Div		
War Diary		01/02/1916	10/02/1916
War Diary	Wormhouldt	11/02/1916	20/02/1916
War Diary	Longaeau	21/02/1916	21/02/1916
War Diary	Berteaucourt	22/02/1916	23/02/1916
War Diary	Gezaincourt	24/02/1916	24/02/1916
War Diary	G. Rullecourt	25/02/1916	29/02/1916
War Diary	Simencourt	01/03/1916	01/03/1916
War Diary	Arras	02/03/1916	05/03/1916
War Diary	Ronville	06/03/1916	14/03/1916
War Diary	Simencourt	15/03/1916	21/03/1916
War Diary	Ronville	22/03/1916	31/03/1916
War Diary	Arras	01/04/1916	30/04/1916
Miscellaneous	From Officers Commdg. 5th (S) Bn. Oxf Bucks Fr Infty	02/06/1916	02/06/1916
War Diary	Arras	01/05/1916	08/05/1916
War Diary	Ronville	09/05/1916	14/05/1916
War Diary	Berneville	15/05/1916	31/05/1916
Miscellaneous	From Officers Commdg. 5th (S) Bn. Oxf Bucks Fr Infty	01/07/1916	01/07/1916
War Diary	Arras	01/06/1916	07/06/1916
War Diary	Ronville	08/06/1916	30/06/1916
Miscellaneous	Proposed Raid On Salient Of Beaurains.	28/06/1916	28/06/1916
Miscellaneous	42nd Inf Bde S 16/16 B.M.	29/06/1916	29/06/1916
Miscellaneous	To-42nd Inf. Bde.	30/06/1916	30/06/1916
Miscellaneous	No. 1 Squad.		
Miscellaneous	14th Divn. G.S. 2371.	30/06/1916	30/06/1916
Miscellaneous	War Diary of Ox & Buck L.I From July 1st to 31st 1916		
Miscellaneous	From Officers Commdg. 5th (S) Bn. Oxf Bucks Fr Infty	01/08/1916	01/08/1916
War Diary	Arras	01/07/1916	31/07/1916
War Diary	Ronville	14/07/1916	21/07/1916
War Diary	Agnez	22/07/1916	29/07/1916
Heading	42nd Brigade. 14th Division. 1/5th Battalion Oxfordshire & Buckinghamshire L. I. August 1916 Attached. Report On Operations 25th August		
Heading	War Diary Of 5th Oxf. & Bucks L. I. 1st-31st Aug 1916		
War Diary	Berneuil	01/08/1916	07/08/1916
War Diary	Buire	08/08/1916	12/08/1916
War Diary	Fricourt	13/08/1916	31/08/1916
Miscellaneous	Narrative Of Operations Of Attack On Delville Wood August 2?th 1916	27/08/1916	27/08/1916
Miscellaneous	Operation Orders.	24/08/1916	24/08/1916
Diagram etc			
Miscellaneous	H 5 Oxs & Bucks Vol II		
War Diary	War Diary Of 5th Bn. Oxfordshire & Buckinghamshire L.I. From September 1st To September 30th, 1916		
War Diary	Epaumesnil	01/09/1916	10/09/1916
War Diary	Albert	11/09/1916	11/09/1916
War Diary	Meaulte	12/09/1916	15/09/1916
War Diary	Montauban	16/09/1916	17/09/1916
War Diary	Camp	18/09/1916	21/09/1916
War Diary	Grand Rullecourt	22/09/1916	24/09/1916
War Diary	Dainville	25/09/1916	26/09/1916

Miscellaneous	Rider		
Miscellaneous	Account Of The Operations 15th September 1916	19/09/1916	19/09/1916
Miscellaneous	Operation Orders.		
Miscellaneous	42 Inf Bde Report On Operation Of Sept 15 1916	15/09/1916	15/09/1916
Map	Montauban		
Operation(al) Order(s)	Appendix "C" To 42nd Inf Bde Operation Order No. 76. Time Table Of Attack	14/09/1916	14/09/1916
Miscellaneous	Time Table Of Attack.		
Heading	5th Oxf & Bucks L. I. From 1st Oct 1916 To 31st Oct 1916		
War Diary	Arras	01/10/1916	29/10/1916
Heading	War Diary Of 5th Oxf & Bucks L. I. From 1st Novr 1916 To 30th Novr 1916 Volume 19		
War Diary	Denier 51c I9	01/11/1916	30/11/1916
Heading	War Diary. Unit. 5th Oxf Bucks L. I. Period From 1-12-16 To 31-12-16 Volume No. 1		
War Diary	Arras	01/12/1916	27/12/1916
War Diary	Trenches	28/12/1916	31/12/1916
Heading	War Diary Unit 5th Oxf & Bucks L. I. Period. From 1st Jan 1917 To 31st Jan 1917		
War Diary		01/01/1917	31/01/1917
Heading	War Diary Unit 5th Oxf & Bucks L. I. Date From 1-2-17 To 28-2-17		
War Diary		01/02/1917	28/02/1917
Heading	War Diary Unit. 5th Oxf & Bucks L. I. Period. From 1.3.17 To 31.3.17		
War Diary		01/03/1917	31/03/1917
War Diary	In The Field	01/04/1917	31/04/1917
Heading	War Diary 5th Oxf & Bucks L I 1 May-31 May 1917		
War Diary		01/05/1917	31/05/1917
Heading	War Diary 5th Oxf & Bucks L.I. 1 June 30 June 1917		
War Diary	In The Field	01/06/1917	30/06/1917
Heading	War Diary. Unit 5th Oxfordshire & Buckinghamshire L. I. Period 1st To 31st July 1917 Volume No 27		
War Diary	Vert Galant	01/07/1917	11/07/1917
War Diary	Meule House	12/07/1917	31/08/1917
War Diary		15/08/1917	20/08/1917
Miscellaneous	From Midnight 23/4th To 3.30 a.m. 25th.		
Miscellaneous	5th. Bn. Oxf. & Bucks. Lt. Infty. Casualties for period 17.8.17 to 24.8.17	24/08/1917	24/08/1917
Heading	War Diary Unit 5th Oxf & Bucks L. I. Period 1st To 30th September 1917 Volume No		
War Diary		01/09/1917	31/10/1917
Heading	War Diary 5th Oxf & Bucks L. I. 1st to 30th November 1917 Volume No.		
Miscellaneous	42nd Inf Bde	01/12/1917	01/12/1917
War Diary		01/11/1917	30/11/1917
Heading	War Diary 5th Oxf & Bucks L. I. December 1917 Volume		
Miscellaneous	42nd Inf Bde	01/01/1918	01/01/1918
War Diary		01/12/1917	31/12/1917
Heading	War Diary 5th Oxf & Bucks L.I. January 1918 Volume		
War Diary		01/01/1918	25/01/1918
Heading	War Diary 5th Oxf & Bucks L. I. February 1918 Volume		
War Diary		01/02/1918	28/02/1918

Heading	14th Division. 42nd Brigade. 5th Battalion Oxford & Bucks Light Infantry March 1918		
War Diary		01/03/1918	31/03/1918
Heading	42nd Inf. Bde. 14th Div. War Diary 5th Battn. The Oxfordshire And Buckinghamshire Light Infantry. April 1918		
War Diary		01/04/1918	30/06/1918
Heading	14th Division 5th Ox & Bucks L. I. Vol I 18-30.5.15 June 18		
War Diary		01/06/1918	20/06/1918

WO 95   1900/4

MAY'15 — JUN'18

5 Bttn Ox & Bucks
          Light Inf

14TH DIVISION
42ND INFY BDE

5TH OXF & BUCKS L.I.
MAY 1915 - JUN 1918

Army Form C. 2118.

WAR DIARY
INTELLIGENCE SUMMARY
(Erase heading not required.)

Instructions regarding War Diaries and Intelligence Summaries are contained in F.S. Regs., Part II. and the Staff Manual respectively. Title pages will be prepared in manuscript.

Place	Date	Hour	Summary of Events and Information	Remarks and references to Appendices
ALDERSHOT	18/5/15		Received Railway Time Table for move of 1st K Train Road	AP
"	19/5/15	8.55 am	1st Train had consisting of 3 officers, 106 other ranks, + all the Regt. Transport, the whole under Major W. WEBB left ALDERSHOT by Troop-train for SOUTHAMPTON, arrived 11.30 am. Transport left at 5 pm + personnel at 7 pm for HAVRE: arrived 7 am + 12 noon respectively, + went into Rest Camp	AP
"	20/5/15		The Remainder of Battn in two Trainloads left ALDERSHOT for FOLKESTONE at 4.20 pm + 4.40 pm respectively. Left FOLKESTONE at 9.30 pm — packet steamer + arrived BOULOGNE 10.30 pm. + went into Rest Camp OSTROHOVE. Spent the day in Rest Camp	AP
BOULOGNE	21/5/15			AP
"	22/5/15	2.30 am	Marched out at 2.30 am + entrained at PONT-DE-BRIQUES Station 3.40 am, in same train with all the Transport of 9th K.R.R: we ought to have had our own Transport Train, + no idea of being Base Camp was wrong	AP
RUBROUCK	10.30 am		Travelled via BOULOGNE, CALAIS, ST OMER, to BAVINCHOVE, where we arrived 10.30 am + detrained. Found all our Transport here. Marched 7 miles to RUBROUCK, where the Battalion went into Billets. The Officers in private houses, the men in barns. Very clean + comfortable Billets. Scarcity of well water is a difficulty.	AP
"	23/5/15		Brigade Route March 7½ miles. The Regt. Machine Gun Officer, + 2 Infantrymen the Bn. Gun Officer went to WISQUES for one days Machine Gun Course. They were shown all the latest advances	AP

Army Form C. 2118

WAR DIARY
INTELLIGENCE SUMMARY

(Erase heading not required.)

Instructions regarding War Diaries and Intelligence Summaries are contained in F. S. Regs., Part II. and the Staff Manual respectively. Title pages will be prepared in manuscript.

Place	Date	Hour	Summary of Events and Information	Remarks and references to Appendices
RUBROUCK	25/5/15		Remained in Billets at RUBROUCK. 1 man admitted Hospital	AP BP
"	26/5/15		Remained in Billets at RUBROUCK. 1 man admitted Hospital.	BP
	27/5/15	12.15 AM	Received orders from Headquarters 42nd INF BDE at 12.15 am to move from RUBROUCK and march to CASSEL. Reveillé 3.30 am. Baggage packed by 4.45 am. Starting point cross roads 2 miles EAST of RUBROUCK. Billetting party of 4 C.Q.M. Strde Lt BLEEK reported to Staff Captain at Starting Point at 5.15 am. Battalion left RUBROUCK at 5.15 am. All ranks with bicycles marched to mile 6.30 am D Coy found the advance guard for the Brigade & marched ½ mile ahead of main body. Passed through CASSEL at 7.55 am. The Batt-n left the rest of the Brigade at the Cross Roads just EAST of CASSEL, & marched on to STEENVOORDE. Total distance marched 12½ miles. Went into Billets in farms on the EAST of the town, the Headquarter Company, Country & 6 officers + 150 other ranks in one farm, A B & D Coys back in one farm, C Coy in two in an area of about ¾ square mile. Very good, clean billets with plenty of straw. All Coys settled in Billets by 11.30 am, & soon after all were connected by telephone with Batt. Hd Qrs. 1000 Rounds of S A A were found by Capt. Shaw Billets left by persons occupant. No 1 K – day	BP
STEENVOORDE	28/5/15		Remained in Billets. Found the Air & Guard of 2 N.C.Os & 9 men left yesterday	

Army Form C. 2118. 3.

WAR DIARY
or
INTELLIGENCE SUMMARY.

(Erase heading not required.)

Place	Date	Hour	Summary of Events and Information	Remarks and references to Appendices
STEEN-VOORDE	29/5/15		Remained in Billets	
	30/5/15		Battalion marched out of billets in STEENVOORDE at 5.25 a.m. Passed the Starting Point, Cross Roads in GODEWAERSVELDE at 6.50 a.m. near Battalion of Brigade. Marched past General Sir Herbert Plumer Commanding the 2nd Army in the square of GODEWAERSVELDE. Marched via BOESCHEPE, MT KOKEREELE, WESTOUTRE, MENIN & HELSTZEVECOTEN, & went into huts in a wood about 1 mile SOUTH of that place at 11.15 a.m. The 9th Rifle Brigade are also here. Drew 1200 rounds of S.A.A. within one of the huts. General Sir Charles Ferguson commanding the 2nd Army Corps visited us in the afternoon. Battalion marched 9 miles; 1 mile out with straining ankle.	

42nd Inf. Bde
14th Div.

5th Battn. The Oxfordshire and Buckinghamshire Light Infantry.

June 1915

(31.5 to 30.6.15)

Attached:
Appendices 1 to 5.
(vis. Report on Operations 22.6.15)

Duplicate

CONFIDENTIAL
=============

WAR DIARY OF
-----ooOoo-----

123rd Canadian Pioneer Battalion, 3rd CANADIAN DIVISION.,

FROM 1st march TO 31st march 1918

-----ooOoo-----

VOLUME 13
=========

WAR DIARY
or
INTELLIGENCE SUMMARY.
(Erase heading not required.)

Army Form C. 2118. 4

5 Post Parks

Instructions regarding War Diaries and Intelligence Summaries are contained in F. S. Regs., Part II. and the Staff Manual respectively. Title pages will be prepared in manuscript.

Place	Date	Hour	Summary of Events and Information	Remarks and references to Appendices
Huts between ZEVECOTEN & LA CLYTTE	31/5/15	9.30 AM	Gen. Sir C. FERGUSSON, G.O.C. 2d Corps addressed this Batt & 9th RIFLE BRIGADE, a fine soldierly speech. Sent to 14th Divn H.Q. 2 N.C.O.s & 3 men as permanent Div & Guard till further orders. Batt paraded 7 pm for improvement of 2d line trenches near KRUISSTRAATHOEK, S.W. of YPRES: started work 10.30 pm & stopped at 1 am, & returned to huts.	BP
"	1/6/15		Worked at night on improving trenches in 2d line. Water is scarce, & difficult to get. The latrine water cart does not stand the jolting caused by pavé roads: must eventually come here, & spite of the fact that the carts are thoroughly overhauled daily, the pumps break up from it. Cart very easily.	BP
"	2/6/15		5 men sent to Brigade for permanent Sanitary duties. Worked at night on improving trenches in 2d line.	BP
"	3/6/15		Worked at night same as last night	
"	4/6/15		Day of rest, no night work.	
"	5/6/15		Machine Gun section marched at 2 pm to LA CLYTTE to DRANOUTRE: under instruction from 138th INF BDE went into trenches occupied by 5th LEICESTERS at 5 pm, for instruction	
"	6/6/15		Batt n left here at 7 am & marched via LA CLYTTE, LOCRE to DETTINGEN huts near DRANOUTRE. A & B Coys went into the trenches with the 4th & 5th LEICESTERS respectively for two days instruction

1577 Wt W10791/1773 500,000 1/15 D. D. & L. A.D.S.S./Forms/C. 2118.

WAR DIARY
INTELLIGENCE SUMMARY

Army Form C. 2118.

Place	Date	Hour	Summary of Events and Information	Remarks and references to Appendices
DRANOUTRE	7/6/15		Instruction in trench warfare: C & D Coy employed in digging communication at night. No 8477 Sgt CUSS & No 10891 Pte SMITH M.G. wounded. Bn H.Q.M. were taken round the trenches of the 4/LEICESTERS. Officers and senior N.C.O. of C & D Coys were lectured by Capt 2d Brigade R.F.A. on co-operation of Arty with Infy & hy 138 INF.BDE Grenade Officer on bombs & had a rifle grenades with practical demonstration.	BP
"	8/6/15		D Coy paraded at 3 PM for work on completion of Communication trench afterwards relieving A Coy in trenches at 8 P.M. C Coy paraded at Hd Qrs of 4th LINCOLNS near LOCRE at 6.50 PM, & with its trenches with the Batt. in relief of B Coy of 5 LEICESTERS. No 11953 Pte STEVENSON R. wounded	BP
"	9/6/15		Reserve Machine Gun Section relieved Service Section in the trenches. Company Sanitary Squads attached to 5/ Div'l Sanitary Section for instruction. Battery Hd Qm. were taken round the trenches of 4/ LINCOLNS. Officers & senior N.C.O's of A & B Coys lectured the same as C & D Coys on 7/6/15. Lt RIDGE-JONES & 2d Lt ESCOTT proceeded ETAPLE, the former as Temporary O.C. details, the latter to escort a draft to Brigade Hd Qrs.	BP
"	10/6/15		Lt MAUDE & 1 N.C.O per Company attended demonstration of efficiency of smoke helmets & respirators at BAILLEUL. B Coy paraded at 1.30 PM & for work on completion of communication trenches, afterwards relieving D Coy in the trenches. A Coy relieved C Coy at 6 P.M. A & B Coys are in for 24 hours	BP

Army Form C.2118.

WAR DIARY
or
INTELLIGENCE SUMMARY.

(Erase heading not required.)

Place	Date	Hour	Summary of Events and Information	Remarks and references to Appendices
DRANOUTRE	11/6/15		Tour of work by Platoons. No 10776 Sgt DONALD.R. slightly wounded. 4" Leicester Regt (T) to whom this Batt⁵ is attached does a raid into an enemy mine, a blown letter up.	App.
"	12/6/15	6.30 am	A + D Cyp returned from trenches preparatory to move of Batt⁵ tomorrow. No 10652 Pte BLUNDY slightly wounded. No 10652 MG section returned from the trenches. Batt⁵ marched at 7 am to LOCRE + went into huts at LA CLYTTE. C.O. + Capt WEBB carried out a reconnaissance E of YPRES with Brigade arrangements.	App.
LA CLYTTE	13/6/15	5 am	Majr WEBB + Capt BARWELL carried out reconnaissance S.E. of YPRES,	App.
"		2 pm	Capts CARFRAE + Lt BERLEIN " " " N.E. " Battalion Intelligence system started under Majr WEBB, for the defence + accurate collection of intelligence.	App.
"	14/6/15	9.15 am	Battalion marched at 9.15 am with 2 minutes interval between each Coy + between the Rear Coy + the Transport. Marched via EVECOTEN + OUDERDOM to huts about 1 mile SW of VLAMERTINGUE: whole of 42ᵈ INF. BDE is concentrated here. Wherever we go we find large quantities of tins (fully left of biscuits) + ammunition (SAA). Early grounds are generally fall. Next duties Dugouts + trenches contracted by Batt⁵ of 9ᵈ NCO i + men arrived from 3 (Reserve) Battalion.	App.

Army Form C. 2118.

WAR DIARY
INTELLIGENCE SUMMARY
(Erase heading not required.)

Place	Date	Hour	Summary of Events and Information	Remarks and references to Appendices
VLAMER-TINGHE	15/6/15		Remained all day in huts. Battalion marched at 10 pm to YPRES & went into trenches S. of LILLE gate at 12.30 am; each man carried 200 rnds S.A.A. & 2 sandbags. Picks & shovels were carried by reliefs. Our artillery fired very heavy fire at 3.30 am on enemy trenches N. of HOOGE, & continued till 6.30 am.	A
	16/6/15	9.50	One at 9.50 am one Coy move out of trenches, & up the Railway Eastwards to some dug outs. he found them occupied by the 9th K.R.R. he then Coy Remained in the Railway embankment. Received orders to send fast at 12 noon & did not move forward till 3.30 pm. Then advanced Eastly by along the Railway across a ridge supposed to be heavy Machine fire, & into a line of trenches S of the MENIN road. While Battalion collected here less C & A Cy, which had moved on up the MENIN road & occupied a different trench N. of it. C.O & self went up to the dilapidly trenches in Rear of this trenches N. of the MENIN road, but found them already full of troops & no room to move them through the Batt & had been ordered to occupy these trenches. C.O & self returned to the Batt & in the trenches S. of MENIN road, & the self then proceeded to the QM of

Army Form C. 2118.

WAR DIARY
or
INTELLIGENCE SUMMARY
(Erase heading not required.)

Instructions regarding War Diaries and Intelligence Summaries are contained in F.S. Regs., Part II. and the Staff Manual respectively. Title pages will be prepared in manuscript.

Place	Date	Hour	Summary of Events and Information	Remarks and references to Appendices
			9 INF BDE & 2nd INF BDE to report on situation & ask for orders. A message was sent to 5 & 6 Coy in advance to retire under cover of darkness & inform Batt. at 8 P.M.	
		8 PM	that Batt. was to retire as soon as possible, & return to huts at VLAMERTINGHE.	
		6.45 PM	This was done at 8.45 am by the same road as Batt. had advanced. The battle site bombardment had been very intense from about 6.45 PM to 8 PM, specially on the trenches S of MENIN road & on the junction of that road & the railway. Evidently with the idea of stopping reinforcements from coming up. 1pt died down at 9 P.M. Casualties killed Lt C.M. BERLEIN. Wounded 2nd Lt CURRY, P.A. & 26 other ranks. Wounded on duty Capt. C.F.K. CARFRAE & 3 other ranks.	NP
VLAMER-	17/6/15		Batt. marched back by Coys to huts & arrived there about 12.30 A.M. Remained there all this day	NPP
TINGHE	18/6/15		Remained in huts. C.O. & 4 Coy Comdrs went out to the trenches N of MENIN road east of YPRES at 3 P.M. They reported to Hd Qrs of the INF BDE the trenches & were little preparation to Batt. occupying the	190

W7476—Wt. W10791/1773 500,000 1/15 D.D. & L. A.D.S.S./Forms/C. 2118.

Army Form C. 2118.

WAR DIARY
or
INTELLIGENCE SUMMARY.

(Erase heading not required.)

Place	Date	Hour	Summary of Events and Information	Remarks and references to Appendices
VLAMER-TINGHE	19/6/15		Remained in huts all day. Draft of 5 O.N.C. Off & men arrived from 3rd Battⁿ. Battⁿ paraded at 7.15 pm & moved off by Coy independently, 100 x between Coys & between the rear Coy & the line Transport: also ammunition, which put in at units carts & battln cart accompanied Battⁿ. Marched along VLAMERTINGHE – YPRES road. Were met by guides from ROYAL SCOTS, whom we were relieving in the trenches. Our first Coy, D Coy reached trenches at 10 P.M.	1970.
		10 PM		
		11 PM	Enemy began to shell communication trench & midway line with shrapnel & gas-shells. Communication trench very bad in places, – blocked by telephone wires.	
		11.30 PM	C. Coy reached trenches, followed by B. & A.	
		1 am	Very heavy rifle & shell fire opened by enemy.	
		2.30 am	Relief completed. Casualties 2ⁿᵈ Lt CRAWFORD & 2ⁿᵈ Lt CLARKE wounded. Killed other ranks 6, wounded 24.	
TRENCHES at RAIL-WAY WOOD E. of YPRES.	20/6/15		Fairly quiet day; occasional shelling & continuous sniping. The trenches are in a very bad condition, deep & narrow with no traverses or dug-outs, & in many places the parapet is not bullet-proof. It is very difficult to get rid of them, as they were originally designed by the Germans to face their own line, & have blocked communication trenches running back towards the enemy.	

1577 Wt.W10791/1773 300,000 1/15 D. D. & E. A.D.S.S./Forms/C. 2118.

WAR DIARY
INTELLIGENCE SUMMARY

Army Form C. 2118.

Instructions regarding War Diaries and Intelligence Summaries are contained in F.S. Regs., Part II. and the Staff Manual respectively. Title pages will be prepared in manuscript.

(Erase heading not required.)

Place	Date	Hour	Summary of Events and Information	Remarks and references to Appendices
	21/6/15	9 p.m.	We have 3 Coys in firing line, 1 in Support. Carrying party of 100 N.C.Os & men under an Officer went down to Brigade H.Q. at L'ECOLE de BIENFAISANCE, where transport carts took rations to trenches: 2 journeys required, & 150 men for this fatigue. It would be better if 2 Battns were left in Reserve who did all the carrying for the two Battns in the trenches: also when the two coys relieve the trenches for each Battn in the front line, one for parties carrying up, & one for those going down. Casualties Killed O.R. 6. Wounded 27.	K.S. Ors BM
	22/6/15		Nothing unusual to record. Attack on enemy redoubt opposite C.5. was proposed, but did not take place, as we had very few bombs. Work on improvement of trenches carried on day & night. Casualties Killed O.R. 1. Wounded O.R. 3. See Appendix 4. Received orders to capture enemy redoubt opposite C.5. tonight: assault was not successful; see orders, report on attack, & plan of trenches attacked. Casualties Killed O.R. 10. Wounded Lt T.M.K. JACKSON, O.R. 52. Missing believed killed 2d Lt T DAVIES, O.R. 9	Appendix 4. Appendix 1, 2 & 3.